Marie A. Ideen

Changing the Crosses and Winning the Crown

Marie A. Ideen

Changing the Crosses and Winning the Crown

ISBN/EAN: 9783337273354

Printed in Europe, USA, Canada, Australia, Japan

Cover: Foto ©Lupo / pixelio.de

More available books at **www.hansebooks.com**

Changing the Crosses

AND

Winning the Crown.

BY

MARIE A. IDEEN.

PHILADELPHIA:
J. B. LIPPINCOTT & CO.
1872.

INTRODUCTORY REMARKS.

DEAR READER,—I wish to introduce this little work, setting it forth to you in great simplicity of style, laying infinitely more weight on the blessed Word of God, as it was delivered to the people of old, so that the plainest mind could comprehend its contents, rather than upon any eloquence or argument of my own. Thus I will picture the Changed Cross, hoping that the more learned of my readers may excuse the humble language in which I present it. I trust, however, dear reader, that you may derive some comfort from it, to strengthen and guide you in bearing the cross until your material life is ended, and you can lay it down at our Saviour's feet, rejoicing that you, in your lifetime, accepted the invitation to come unto Him, which is given to all. This, I hope, may be your portion, and then to enjoy that heavenly rest, after carrying the cross and exchanging all the sorrows and privations of life into joys everlasting.

CONTENTS.

	PAGE
CHAPTER I	9
CHAPTER II	31
CHAPTER III	43
CHAPTER IV	57
CHAPTER V	66
CHAPTER VI	78
THE CROSS	114
THE CROSS-BEARER	115
THE CROWN	116
THE PALM OF VICTORY	118
THE WEDDING GARMENT	119
THE CELESTIAL CITY	120

Changing the Crosses

AND

Winning the Crown.

CHAPTER I.

In the mansions of heaven
We shall find rest. Seek the road
That leadeth there; and remember
The Cross and the Crown:
It is the cross-bearer that shall be crowned.

In the mansions of heaven
The crosses will cease. Let us carry them
Faithfully till there we have reached;
Then in harmony with angels bright
We shall find they will welcome us
Into our rest.

AT Nature's beautiful shrine we stoop to gather flowers to adorn the cross we wish to carry; but there is one who bids us come unto Him, and take up our cross daily and follow in his footsteps; and He invites all to come that are weary and heavy-laden, and says, "I will give you rest. Take my yoke upon you, and learn of me;" "for my yoke is easy and my burden is light."

These, my dear reader, are the words of our blessed Master, who bids us come to Him and change crosses. He knew that no one could find heaven by carrying a cross of flowers. No; we must lay it down and take up the one that our Saviour offers, and that will be the chosen of God for every child that wishes to go to that beautiful heaven which St. Paul speaks of, "the glory of which never entered into man's heart to conceive." We must listen to what the Saviour has said when He bids us all come unto him,—He that was meek and lowly of heart.

And that we may exchange crosses with our Saviour, we must first be willing to take up the cross that comes daily, and not be troubled what kind of a cross it is. We children of earth desire to carry crosses that have no wreaths of sorrow around them, and we desire to adorn them with all that would make our life happy. But such crosses will not lead us in the way to heaven. Let us consider well what we have to do as cross-bearers, journeying that way,—the way to the city of peace, where dwell the holy ones, the redeemed of earth, who are spoken of in Revelation, vii. 14, as having come out of great tribulation.

As I am one of the cross-bearers of the exchanged cross, I will, in the first place, inform you that I once loved to carry the cross of flowers; but its beauty faded, and I am thankful to God that He showed me the difference between the two crosses; and I wish you to become acquainted with the nature and quality of each.

In the first place, let me carry you to one of the heights of earthly delights before we descend together into the garden of sorrow, and there learn how to reach the summit of heavenly blessedness. Then I shall invite you to sit with me in misfortune's shade, for I shall have words to say which may prove useful to you in your own subsequent experience; but first we will go in our thoughts, if you will follow me, in the past when I carried the flowery cross. Not a withered blossom was on its breast. It was adorned with the choicest flowers; its name was that of love's token of uninterrupted joys and worldly happiness of every kind.

I thought that those flowers could never wither; but oh, when they commenced to be wet with sorrow's dew, then I saw the leaves shrivel up and the blossoms droop, as a token that they were dying with sorrow and blighted hopes! Then I thought this cross I cannot bear any more with comfort; all is so dark and desolate within and without; another I must have to console my woe. But, as I sought for another, and again for another, I found that all had their thorns and thistles among the flowers; and so, at last, a voice spoke to my saddened heart, "Seek not to cull the flowers of earth; stoop not to pluck them; for they will all wither, and the garlands that you have twined for their adornment will only whisper sadness in their fragrance. But come and follow me. I will lead you in ways that shall enrapture your soul; and then in heavenly harmony you shall find angels that will show you the garden of Paradise, where the cross-bearers of earth's flowery crosses can exchange them for the beautiful flowers of heaven, that grow by the clear streams of Paradise, and invite every wayfaring child of earth to come up higher and higher, to see their beauty."

Oh, there is beauty unspeakable and full of glory, to which you are invited! You must learn how all things work together for good, even if your cross seem heavy. Remember, that there was One who suffered and died that you might be saved, if you will follow in his footsteps. He speaks to you in tender tones, "Come, follow me;" and He will lead you to streams of living purity, where you shall taste the delights of the upper sanctuary.

Dear reader, we are to mount the summit of perfection by going through sorrow's garden, and there pluck the immortal flowers that grow by the wayside of despair, suffering disappointments of numerous kinds. To this all are invited who wish to become bearers of the cross that our Saviour offers.

Oh, come, ye children of earth, and let this console you, that peace shall be your portion; for the Master said, " My peace I give unto you; not as the world giveth give I unto you." "And I shall pray my Father for you, that your faith shall not fail." So we have one that has shown us how we are to reach that heaven of peace where dwell the righteous of the Lord.

And now, as we give ourselves up to follow the Master, we shall be guided and protected into a pure and holy way, for He assures us that He is "the Way, the Truth, and the Life."

Now, if we make up our minds to follow Him wheresoever He goeth, we shall find that we are in the way that leadeth to heaven. He also said, "I am the Light of the world." And if we follow that Light, we cannot walk in darkness. We must be willing to accept his precepts, and to bid farewell to all the flowery crosses of earth, remembering that we have set out for heaven, and if we have no cross we cannot have the crown; and the greater the cross, the brighter will be the crown. May we be able, as we pass through this earth's weary pilgrimage, to learn the lessons of redeeming love, that we may not only be purified from sin ourselves, but be able to purify each other, feeling that we have a duty to perform to our neighbor as well as to ourself; and, like our Saviour, may we be able to say, "My yoke is easy and my burden is light!" He said, "I come to do the will of my Father;" and we are his friends if we do whatsoever He commanded us.

We have all a duty to perform to each

other, to ourselves, and to our God. But we must, first of all, take up our cross daily, and follow the Saviour; we must be pure in heart, pure in mind, and give up all that corrupts soul and body, feeling that, without holiness, "no one shall see God."

May you, my readers, all feel in unison with me in thinking it is delightful to ascend the mount of God, even if it leads through sorrow's garden. We must not forget the garden and the cross. The cross is reared in sorrow's garden, in harmony with the divine teaching, and we shall all find that it is heavy, unless we do the will of the Master, who has carried it before us, to cheer and brighten our way by his divine example. He says, "Ye cannot be my disciples except ye keep my commandments;" "He it is that loveth me who loveth his brother." And by this we know that we have passed from death unto life, because we love the brethren. "He that loveth not his brother abideth in death." Now it is not sufficient that we carry our own crosses, but we have to help to carry those of others also. He says, "Love one another, as I have loved you."

"In my Father's house are many mansions; if it were not so I should have told you." We are to prepare our hearts and make them ready for the holy ones to dwell in, so that the Father and the Son can come and take up their abode in them. We must be willing to be regenerated, and free from all that pollutes the soul and the body; and thus our hearts will become fit temples for the holy ones to dwell in. Love one another, and so fulfill the whole law of Christ, as it reads in Galatians, v. 14. We are to look to God for wisdom in all that pertains to our own and others' temporal and spiritual welfare. Thus we fulfill the whole law.

How different modern Christianity is in comparison with that of Christ and the Apostles! He says, "If ye love me, keep my commandments, and teach men to do likewise." That shows to us that we must not only keep them ourselves, but we must impart them to others also. Therefore, those who do not keep the Master's command must commence in earnest, and for their very lives, while time is given them to accept the offer of mercy. Work while it is day, for the night cometh, when no man can work; plant and sow in the right time the heavenly seeds of his teaching, in the garden of your heart, that every day you live you may have fruit to the glory of God, to show to the world that the seed has taken root. Christ said, " In this is my Father glorified, that ye bear much fruit." John, xv. 8. So we must all in unison try to be true followers of Christ, and take up his cross daily, that we may be faithful witnesses of his suffering, remembering that if we do not suffer with Him we cannot reign with Him. This is a very different path to that of walking on roses and carrying the flowery cross. Let us be faithful to our high calling in Jesus Christ, and neither look to right nor left for any worldly comfort; but march forward to the mark of perfection, realizing that there is a prize to be gained, and only as we can lay down the attire of worldliness and worldly pleasures, putting on the armor of God and fighting manfully to establish the household of God, can we help to form the kingdom of heaven upon earth as it is in heaven.

Has it ever occurred to you who read these pages how God's kingdom is to be established upon the earth, and his will be done on earth as it is in heaven? Heaven's first law is order; that is, we must recognize that we are living under the laws of heaven, although man in his ignorance does not realize the laws that govern his inner nature; but when he desires to do good, evil is present. We ought to live to elevate our better nature, and we must be willing to become what our Saviour has commanded us to be. We shall be, as He says, "his friends," if we do whatsoever He has told us to do.

In order that we may learn to know his

teachings fully, we must do as He said, "Search the Scriptures," for they do testify of Him; and we must feel that we are compelled to take up his life in our life to be his true followers. He never set forth in his teachings that we should have nothing to do but think of Him and call upon his name. He says, Not every one that saith unto me Lord, Lord, shall enter *into* the kingdom of heaven; but he that doeth the will of my Father which is in heaven." Matthew, vii. 21. He says, also, "I came to do the will of Him that sent me, and ye are my friends if ye do whatsoever I have commanded you."

We cannot be his chosen disciples if we do not follow the Saviour. We ought to fall so in love with the character of Christ that we shall have it for our daily meditation, exclaiming, from our innermost soul, like the man spoken of in the Word (Luke, ix. 57, 58), who was so in love with Christ that he said, "Lord, I will follow thee whithersoever thou goest." To this Christ answered, "Foxes have holes, and birds of the air have nests; but the Son of man hath not where to lay his head." This, perhaps, will be our portion if we, like that man, desire to follow the Master. But let us remember that we are, all of us here below, only on a journey, and soon the weary pilgrimage shall be over; and then it is well to have laid up treasures where neither rust nor moth destroy. Let us be of the number that do not live for this world; but while we live in it let us make right use of it, and seek out the poor, the destitute, that have no homes nor any comforts on their journey, and carry to them the glad tidings of redeeming love, and help those who are in need.

Christ knew that his followers could not have much of this world's goods, because if we wish to carry the same cross that He did, we must sympathize with each other, and distribute our goods to each other as the suffering stand in need of them. Acts, ii. 45.

Dear reader, what does it matter for the

little time we are here on this earth, even if we should be deprived of all worldly enjoyments? Let us try in earnest, and see how near we can come into those steps that we are commanded to follow. Remember, it is impossible to walk in the footsteps of our Saviour if we are not willing to carry the cross, for surely there is a cross for us to bear all the way through life. But when we think that He, whose every breath was human love, tells us to follow, can you hesitate to obey the command and willingly to lay down your flowery cross and exchange it for the one He offers? Oh, could we all realize how glorious it is to be a true cross-bearer of our Saviour, and feel his holy spirit whispering to us, " Be of good cheer, I have overcome the world," how unspeakably blessed would be our lot both here and hereafter!

He said, " In the world ye shall have tribulation; but in me ye shall have peace."

Oh, that peace on our pilgrimage that soothes every troubled wave in our breast and leaves a quiet calm! This is what we need. Without this we cannot bear up under the heavy crosses of life that we have to carry; but if we are willing, we shall find that we are not alone on our pilgrimage; for Christ said, when He left his Apostles, that it was expedient that He should go; for if He did not go, the Comforter would not come. And mark what follows. When He comes "He will guide you into all truth;" "He shall not speak of Himself; but whatsoever He shall hear, that shall He speak, and He will show you things to come." Now, let us look at these words, written in John, xvi., and see if we can gain any light to our understanding.

It appears that this Comforter, the spirit of truth that Christ spake about as to come, is something more besides the Legacy, that is to say, the Word, that was left for our instruction. As He said, there is another spirit to come, even the spirit of truth, to each one of us, and He is to declare what He hears, and guide us into all truth. This opens a new channel through which we are to discover the hidden things of God. He will speak to us of what He hears, and that will be truth, because Christ said we should be led into all truth, through this spirit. Now, let us reflect upon the remarks presented, and learn what our Saviour says. It "was expedient that He should go, otherwise this spirit could not come." "And when He comes He shall reprove the world of sin, because He went to the Father." Now, this holy spirit, the spirit of truth, that is to accomplish this mighty work in us, is that spirit that vibrates through the whole angelic host; and as we become imbued with this spirit, we can enter into rapport with those holy ministering spirits which we read of in Hebrews, i. 14; ii. 15, "that is sent to minister unto them who shall be heirs of salvation," and Psalm xci.: "The great God has given his angels charge over us, to keep us in all our ways, and hold us up in their hands." And the whole Bible speaks in its records of such visitations to mortals. These good and holy ones will lead us every moment of our life, if we will be led and guided by them. The Word declares that "they are sent to minister to those that shall be heirs of salvation;" "And how shall we escape if we neglect so great salvation?" We are to give heed to all this, not to make light of it, and shut the door on these glorious lights that were sent by the Father to come and guide mortals in the way they are to go. And if we ourselves cannot comprehend how we are to be guided by these ministering spirits that are to bear witness of Christ, let us see and learn of those that have the gift to understand what they bear to us in their sacred mission. Christ had angels ministering to Him; and should we be above their ministration, when He that was perfect needed their presence? May God help us to comprehend the Father's love towards us all, who says He has sent his angels to lead us in our ways!

Now, we, all of us, need to feel in our innermost, if not gifted with outward vision, that those angels guard us; and, as the Word teaches, "There is more joy in heaven over one sinner that repenteth, than over ninety and nine just persons who need no repentance." Let us look at this in its true light. It shows us that angels know all that befall sinners on their journey of life; and we can see, or ought to see by this, how necessary it is so to live and act that we can have them for our company, and know they have joy in their heavenly mansions because a sinner has repented.

Oh, friends, let us have this picture continually before our eyes, — the changed cross; for by this change only can we cause joy in heaven. How necessary, then, it is for us to cease sinning, and try to live a life of purity, that we may blend with those heavenly inhabitants that visit us daily, watching over us for our welfare, surrounding our dwellings, that the destroyer cannot come near unto us! But this can only be as we desire above everything to be pure, perfect, and holy in all things: then those heavenly guards can visit us. But if we, on the other hand, live a life of sin and abomination, contrary to the life and teachings of Christ, then we cannot expect that we can attract those heavenly messengers; but, instead, we draw evil spirits, that pollute us with vices of every kind, and establish themselves within us until they become the rulers of our lives.

I speak as one having some authority in these matters, for I am not unacquainted with the vices and plans of the destroyer, and how he seeks to entrap the soul through human agency; but I have tasted of life's bitter cup, and I can assure you it pays you, even while in earth-life, to set out to be a Christian.

Out of evil cometh good; so we must never think there is no help for us; neither that God is so merciful that it does not matter how we live, or that Christ died for us, and all will be right. This reasoning will not do for a man's salvation. We read in Phil. ii. 12, 21, that we are to work out our own salvation with fear and trembling; seeking the things which are Jesus Christ's, and walking after the pattern set before us of Him. This is what we have to do while traveling through this pilgrimage, if we would gain heaven. Who would like to live always away from heaven, —that beautiful home? Let us reason, and see how great God's love is to us. He has given us all that we need on this earth; everything grows for food and raiment for the body. All things are provided by a kind and loving Father, who says, "If your earthly father and mother forsake you, I will take you up." Oh, let us not forget to lift up our hearts to this Father; and each time that we share the bounties of his love in food, drink, or raiment, or anything that is supplied to the needs either of body or soul, let us not be ashamed, as so many are in this day of general unbelief, to thank Him for his bounties. He tells us that we must not take any thought for to-morrow, for to-morrow will take care of itself; and He has taught us to seek first the kingdom of God and his righteousness, and all the rest shall be given unto us.

This, no doubt, seems strange to many, but nevertheless it is true, that if we use the faculties for our support that God has given to us, we shall have what we need. And if the day sometimes seems cloudy, as though his countenance was withdrawn, and seemingly He had forgotten us, let us remember that He hides Himself only for a season, and at such times there will be a trial of our faith. But no one has ever yet been confounded that put his trust in the Lord. He is a safe refuge, if we live in his laws and follow in his precepts. We can never have a better friend, for He is a friend at all times and under all circumstances, and to love Him we must enter into communion with Him, as a child with a kind father. He will hear us, if we come in the right way.

When we first awake in the morning, we are to think of our heavenly Father, and pray to Him, that He will keep us from sinning, and make us pure in heart, that all our dealings may please Him. And then we must also remember that we have a duty to our fellow-men who travel with us through this pilgrimage. They need a consoler as well as ourselves. Let us speak words of cheer to each other; and may we feel that life thereby is made better. And, as the Word teaches in I. John, iv. 20, "He that loveth not his brother whom he hath seen, how can he love God whom he hath not seen?" So, however poor, sinful, and degraded, let us, as far as we can, get rid of our own sins,—pride and corruption; try to be the ones to redeem, comfort, and help each other while we are on the way, that we may all become a purified band of Christ's followers, and our Father may say to us at the journey's end, "These are my beloved sons and daughters, in whom I am well pleased!"

CHAPTER II.

> If with thorns and thistles
> Thy pathway be strewed,
> Remember the walks of Paradise
> Are strewed with flowers.

TO this thorny road we will, in the first place, direct our attention; and, as we travel on its piercing thorns, we must remember that we form blossoms of heavenly beauty to adorn the path of Paradise. None can enter in there on those glorious walks without first having trod among the thistles of the earth.

Let us see what those thistles consist of. We are wandering hither and thither, seeking life's flower-strewed path. But here we must say with the Psalmist, "All is vanity and vexation of spirit;" and mortals cannot find them as lasting roads. Those of you that are destined to heaven must carry the cross, and often a heavy one; not of rare beauties, but such as the most of us would shrink from. Dear friends, as you commence to be cross-bearers of the cross that Christ offers, you must look to God, from whence cometh our help, and remember that He has promised that He will never forsake us, but be with us to the end. We shall find, in so doing, that we shall have sufficient strength to carry our crosses; and if thorns and thistles pierce our feet while here in this valley of grief, and often, as though the weary traveler were enwrapped with the clouds of affliction, let us remember there will be sunrise of joy on resurrection morning. So, if life is ever so cheerless, let us not be discouraged or downhearted, but make up our minds to this effect, that if the whole of life's pathway should be strewn with thorns and thistles, we will carry our crosses, God and his holy angels that are sent helping us. To this we must try to say,

Amen, and march forward, remembering that there is a prize to be gained.

Heaven rejoices over every traveler that has set out for the celestial city,—the place of the living God, where dwell the faithful children of the Most High. May we be able to reach that holy place of uninterrupted happiness! To be able to reach that place, we must give up all that bewilders the senses with the pride of the flesh and lust of the eye,—desiring nothing higher than to be endowed with purity of heart; longing after nothing but what will make us heavenly and divine.

If these be our wishes, we shall be helped and assisted, and be able, as the Word teaches, to work out our own salvation.

Angels help us, because they are sent from our Father to teach us; and if we only try to live a pure, holy, and sacrificing life, they will help us in all that pertains to our true happiness in this life and the life to come.

We are their pupils, because God has, as we read in Heb. i. 14, sent them to minister to those that shall be heirs of salvation, and to hold us up in all our ways. And if we desire to be like angels, and dwell with them eternally, we shall have a crown on our forehead and a palm of victory in our hands.

Oh, dear reader, is this not worth while carrying the cross for a little longer, and then in rapturous delight enjoy such a heaven of bliss for evermore?

To this you are invited, and for this purpose the angels are sent to teach you and beckon you heavenward, — to come home; and, while on earth, to prepare for that home. Yes, let us give more earnest heed to the things spoken of by angels, that when the time comes we can lay down our crosses and take up the crown and the palm. May we be the blessed souls that have followed the teachings of those that have been sent to us for our instruction; and then be able, in unison with them, to celebrate the joys in heaven over sinners that have repented; and may each one of us feel that we belong to that number that have gained redemption through the repentance from sin. Hoping, my reader, that we all may have a desire to live a pure life, free from sin, and advance towards perfection until we have given up all that is contrary to the laws and statutes of God.

It is necessary that we should drink of life's bitter cup; for if we have not tasted of its bitterness, how can we realize Christ's sayings to those in St. Mark, x. 38, who ask of Him to have it granted unto them to sit with Him in his glory? To which He answered them, "Ye know not what ye ask. Can ye drink of the cup that I drink of? and be baptized with the baptism that I am baptized with?" And they answered Him, "We can." Then Jesus said unto them, "Ye shall indeed drink of the cup that I drink of; and with the baptism that I am baptized withal shall ye be baptized."

That shows us, according to these words, that we cannot enter heaven without drinking the bitter cup, and being baptized with the baptism of sorrow. Oh, that we may reflect upon this as we ought to, not forgetting that we are travelers of a day, and know not if another day, month, or year shall be granted unto us!

Let us, then, be up and doing, — a heart ready for any trial of faith that the great God in his providence has ordained for us. May we feel that our heavenly Father doeth all things well!—and if we only put our trust in Him, we shall find that our life will glide on with inward peace, such as this world cannot give, because this world's comforts are at most but vanity and vexation of spirit. Nothing is worth living for but that only which fits and prepares us to join the heavenly company that has passed through the valley and shadow of death, and now enjoy life everlasting.

For, to reach those heavenly inhabitants, we must be willing to empty the cup of bitterness, carrying our crosses, however heavy they may be; remembering "that afflictions, if properly received, shall work out a far more exceeding weight of glory than this world ever could bestow upon us." This is what is promised to those that become purified through affliction's heavy yoke. Then, again, we have Christ's words, "Come unto me, all ye that labor and are heavy laden, and I will give you rest;" for He says, "My yoke is easy and my burden is light," and "learn of me, for I am meek and lowly of heart." Oh, what a blessed invitation,—that we can come, at any time, to learn such sublime lessons of humiliation and comfort! Let this console you, oh, weary pilgrim, on life's journey,—that He trod the same path that He wishes you to travel!

He says that we must follow in his footsteps; that comes very close to his suffering; and when we commence to realize that it is only through suffering, deprivation, and self-sacrifice that we are to be made perfect, then how necessary it is for us to do all in our power to be like Christ!—not to follow the road of sin and pleasure any longer, if we are now on that road; but give it up, and set out for heaven,—that beautiful home, where sorrows and trials are unknown, and all shall whisper peace forever.

Oh, try to endure life's vicissitudes with the meekness of a Saviour's love! He knew what it was to empty the bitter cup of affliction, and He knew how to sympathize with us, in having to take up our cross daily, as He said we must in order to follow Him. And we read of Christ teaching the rich man, in St. Mark, x. 17-21, who came to ask of Him what he should do to inherit eternal life. Note the answer that Christ gave the rich man! "Thou knowest the commandments, Do not commit adultery, Do not kill, Do not steal, Do not bear false witness, Defraud not, Honor thy father and mother." To this the rich man answered, "Master, all these have I observed from my youth." Then Christ in particular said to him, "One thing thou lackest: go thy way, sell whatsoever thou hast, and give to the poor, and thou shalt have treasure in heaven: and come, take up the cross and follow me."

Just think of the sacrifice that is required of each one of us, in this life, as we journey along, often unconcerned of the steps we ought to take to go in the road that leads heavenward! And, according to this teaching of the Master, we must admit that the road which the Christian pilgrim has to walk is a hard one; and before we become imbued with Christ's love in the heart, we must often feel like the rich man of old, and turn away grieved from such a thorny path, and rather seek another, and go to heaven our own way. But I ask the reader to think of these words of Christ, that "no one could come unto the Father except through Him," and consequently that none can inherit heaven, where God dwells, except through Him. How necessary, then, to begin to prepare in earnest to learn how to approach the Father through Christ! This cannot be accomplished by having a blind faith, which works no righteousness; but by unwavering faith in the promise that if we follow in the footsteps of the Master, as we are commanded to do, we shall come to the Father thereby.

We have Christ's words in St. Matthew, vii 21–24, "Not every one that saith unto me, Lord, Lord, shall enter into the kingdom of heaven; but he that doeth the will of my Father, which is in heaven."

It is impossible to think that we can comprehend the Father, or do his will, except we are willing to be true followers of the Saviour's teaching. We have to come to Him, not in faith only, but in living examples, such as He has set forth to us through his exemplary life. Through this process commences a true Christian's pilgrimage on earth. And when we make up our minds to follow Christ, in keeping his words, and fulfilling his commandments, then the Father will love us, and Christ and the Father will come and make their abode with us. Thus we become one with them, as we read in St. John, xvii.

21, "That they all may be one; as thou, Father, art in me, and I in thee, that they also may be one in us: that the world may believe that thou hast sent me."

How delightful to think that there was one that was willing to suffer and die, that if we are willing to adopt his precepts we shall be saved! Oh, that we may get that living faith that will cleanse our hearts from all evil and unbelief! believing that all things are possible to those that believe; and as Christ assures us in St. John, xiv. 12, "He that believeth on me, the works that I do shall he do also; and greater works than these shall he do; because I go unto my Father."

Let us commence to realize that we are placed here on earth, one generation after another, to work out the Lord's glorious teachings, until each one of us can crucify the lust of the eye, the lust of the flesh, and the pride of the world, and in Christ's precepts dwell.

Oh, let us pray for this holy baptism that

will make us pure within and without, so that wherever we go we may benefit others by the blessed influences proceeding from us, and we may go hand-in-hand with all that is heavenly and sublime!

May God help us to do his will on earth as it is done in heaven, for his own glory and for the benefit of each other, that we may be fully able to realize the meaning of these words in I. John, iv. 20, "He that loveth not his brother whom he hath seen, how can he love God whom he hath not seen?"

CHAPTER III.

*There is a road that leads to God,—
Love to humanity is its name;
It teaches us that no one can come
Unto God without following
In the Master's steps.*

WE will now reflect a little concerning this road,—how we are to follow Him, closer and closer, until He becomes our entire pattern, and we are so enrapt with his beautiful teachings, that his life becomes our life, and that the human love which beamed forth from his beautiful soul may be our portion. Oh, thou fount of God's love! how thy soul was refreshed daily with the divine strength and healing balm of God's love! It was because He was willing to do his Father's will; and in so doing He became the recipient of all that was divine.

Oh, that we all were more perfect, and could understand the sacredness of his mission and its bearing to us when He said, "I come to do my Father's will;" and that "we are his friends if we do whatsoever He bids us!" Let us not pass this by, thinking we have nothing to do, and that He had only to come and do his Father's will, and so save us, while we do nothing for our own salvation. Remember, He says "we must follow in his footsteps." And, to follow after Christ, we certainly, one and all, have to carry out our Father's will, only with this difference, that He had the Father's image formed in his heart; and we must walk after the pattern set before us by Him, till He can be formed in us, the hope of glory. The closer we live up to his precepts, the easier it will be for us to follow Him.

Then, as we pass through the garden of sorrow, we shall be refreshed, as the woman of Samaria that accepted of the living water that Christ offered to her, as we read in John iv. that she met with Jesus when she came to draw water from Jacob's well. Jesus being there, wearied with his journey, sat by the well, and saith unto her, "Give me to drink," and informed her, "whosoever drinketh of this water shall thirst again. But whosoever drinketh of the water that I shall give him shall never thirst; but the water that I shall give him shall be in him a well of water springing up into everlasting life." "She saith unto him, Sir, give me this water that I thirst not." "Jesus saith unto her, Go and call thy husband, and come hither." She was desirous of having this living water which is the gift and power of the love of God in the soul, that purifies from all iniquity.

We read in verses 8, 9, that she "left her water-pot and went away into the city, and saith to the men, Come, see a man which told me all things that ever I did: is this not the Christ?" She wanted to proclaim to them that she had found a pearl of great price from the depth of that pure, gushing fountain of love, which is Christ.

Thus we shall find there will be many resting-places where we can be refreshed from this fountain, and where we can sit down under the pleasant shade of Christ's love and the angels' wings. Oh, let us, while we rest in this garden, meditate on all that constitutes the blossoms of this garden!

The garden of Gethsemane was to our Saviour a cheerless place; and, if we take up our cross daily, we cannot expect to escape our Gethsemane. But it is delightful to think that He had angels that ministered to Him in his lonely hours. No human being was there, according to record. So it is with us, dear reader. Often, when we pass through the garden of sorrow, we have no one to cheer us on the way. We do not often meet with perfect followers of Christ that minister to mortals and sympathize with them as Christ did, although He said, "Love one another, as I have loved you."

In such a case it is well to realize the

blessed angels that are sent to minister unto us and hold us up in our ways. We can be sure of their presence, even if all earthly friends forsake us; for if this was not a fact, God's words in many places in the holy Scriptures would be an untruth, together with human experience at the present time.

May we be able to realize the King in his beauty, and how He comes, in his second coming, with his holy angels, to judge the world in righteousness! And, with the help of the Father, and all the holy angels that are sent, may we comprehend their mission and the glorious testimony of Christ, to which they bear witness! May we be able to receive those glorious messengers, and to feel it a sacred delight to be favored with their visits of redeeming love; for Christ is coming in the clouds of our understanding with those that are sent to judge the world! Those messengers, when they come, teach us to pray and how to follow in the Master's footsteps.

Now, it appears, since Christ suffered, that most people think that they have nothing to observe as followers of Christ and worshipers of God but to keep the Sabbath, attend church, and, perhaps, listen to a good or a bad sermon, as they may fancy it to be; thinking after that they have nothing else to do for God, for themselves, or their neighbors, because Christ has done all for them; and that all we have to do is to believe this with steadfast faith and all shall be right. This is as far as religion is practiced in these days, with few exceptions.

What are we to do in this case? some would say. Dear reader, to commence to live a religion such as the Master Jesus Christ hath set forth in his doctrine, we must, first of all, accept the law, which is the new commandment that He gave to his disciples: "A new commandment I give unto you, that you love one another, as I have loved you." St. John, xiii. 34.

It seems that what Christ tried to do through

his beautiful teachings and exemplary life, was to impress on the minds of the people that all the coming generations should be blessed by adopting his precepts. He knew that unless this commandment was lived out, we could not be like Him. He was the new covenant through whom we all have to enter to become endowed with the power of his love to enable us to keep that new commandment.

Let us see what we have to do to carry it out. It certainly cannot be done by a faith that does not work love; for if such a faith can free us from sin, and induce us to do such deeds as He commands us to perform (Matt. xxv.), namely, "To feed, clothe, and comfort our neighbor in sickness," bereavement, and despair with that same love as He had, then it would be a different world to what it is at present.

Now, to begin with, whether we profess or do not profess to be Christians, it is time that all of us both profess and possess this pure and undefiled religion,—the only one He ever introduced,—which follows, as a matter of course, after the new commandment has been adopted; and that is, "To visit the fatherless and widows in their afflictions, and to keep ourselves unspotted from the world." This is what is called pure religion. James, i. 27.

Now, let us see if that corresponds with the religion of the present day; whether that glorious command of our Saviour has become a law in every one's heart that professes to be a follower of Christ, his, and the Apostles' teachings. We read in I. John, iii. 17, "That whoso hath this world's good, and seeth his brother have need, and shutteth up his bowels of compassion from him, how dwelleth the love of God in him?"

How many are followers of Christ, if we judge them by these sayings? By this we see we must not love in words, but in deed and in truth. James teaches, in ii. 26, "For as the body without the spirit is dead, so faith without works is dead also."

If we seek in the blessed Word of God for

the record of those that every Christian creed hangs upon for instruction, let us commence to seek right, and for the right things, that we may be profited unto salvation. We shall then find that the blessed Word teaches different things from what is practiced at the present day by the professed followers of Christ. No one is willing to drink the bitter cup that He drank, although He declares that we must drink of the same cup and be baptized with the same baptism wherewith He was baptized before we can enter into his Father's kingdom.

How many professed Christians believe this? We all like too well to carry the flowery crosses whose fragrance delights the senses with intoxicating odor. Oh, this is what professors of religion, *and others*, most like to carry, instead of the cross of Christ, which we must carry in order to follow in his footsteps!

>   As we take up the cross of Christ,
>   And follow in his steps,
>   The flowery cross to us
>   Will cease to be a delight.

Dear reader, we must have an experience of those words before we can realize them in our hearts. We cannot be Christians until their fulfillment is accomplished in our life. It seems while we carry the flowery crosses, serving the world with heart and soul, and laying up treasures on earth, instead of in heaven, that the cross of Christ is, to the carnal mind, a heavy burden,—that is, while we seek to lay up treasures on earth; and we see no beauty in the cross, only as a heavy burden. Some of us know from experience that those feelings are realities, and will be so while the human heart is unregenerated.

But as soon as we commence to see the beauty of Christ's divine love and sacrifices for humanity, and begin to realize his beautiful mission in its true light, feeling that we cannot be a partaker of his love and affection in our hearts while we stand isolated and alone,—dead, as it were, in trespasses and sins, and absolutely dead to all that is of a quickening and a life-giving power: as long as this is the case with us, and we cannot comprehend the beautiful character of Christ so as to have a desire to blend with Him, so long we are carnally dead, and can have no fellowship with Him.

He said, if we love Him we should keep his commandments. Now, to serve and love Christ, we must fall in love with the cross that He wishes us to carry. He knew that we could not be cross-bearers of the cross He offers as long as we have chosen the cross that belongs to this world's enjoyments.

We never shall be able to exchange crosses with our Saviour until we make up our minds first that it is necessary to take all things that the flowery cross consists of and go to Him and lay it down at his feet, and make a burial there, and resolve that if we have to sacrifice everything that we ever loved that belongs to this world, we will make a sacrifice, and profit thereby. As St. Paul says in II. Cor. iv. 17, "For our light affliction which is but for a moment worketh for us a far more exceeding and eternal weight of glory."

Now, if we reflect for a moment that we must be willing to become cross-bearers with Christ, so that we desire nothing higher than to be in his company, we must go hand in hand in this human redemption; for as He said He was the way, then most certainly we have to follow in that way. No one, He said, shall walk in darkness, if they keep in the way that He has shown us through his examples; neither shall we go astray, but follow wheresoever He goeth.

My dear reader, it is impossible for mortals to carry the cross of Christ alone: we must have power from on high to help us on our pilgrimage. May God help us all; and may we be willing to do all in our power to assist each other to carry our crosses! Now, if we could only be the servant in whom God was well pleased; but to be acceptable to God, we have to sacrifice everything, and be willing to do and suffer anything, and thus fulfill the law of Christ. We are to be endowed with power from on high, so as to be able to carry out the principles of Christ. And He said, "As many as would He gave the power to become the sons of God."

May the Holy Spirit enlighten us what to do to serve God! O Father, thou that knowest the struggles of mortals, help us to endure! We are left here on earth to work out our own salvation, and only as we can endure faithfully unto the end can we realize the benefit of bearing the cross. Christ carried his cross daily, and we must remember his love and forbearance, realizing, while we carry our crosses, that we must be willing to do as He did,—to suffer anything for righteousness' sake. We must live a life to the glory of God, through kind deeds of charity and benevolence to humanity, thus feeling that we have a high priest who is acquainted with all our infirmities,—that suffered like unto our own suffering.

O thou who seest mortals, have mercy upon us all, and help us to carry our crosses; and when we seem to faint under the burden and peculiar trials that we have to pass through, may we have strength to endure to the end! Help us, O God! and to thee shall be the glory for ever and ever. Amen.

CHAPTER IV.

> Through sorrow often we become
> Initiated into heaven's throng;
> And only as we can appreciate
> Their teachings, can we realize
> The healing balm of heaven.

THUS, my dear reader, we will reflect on the garden of sorrow, and how many weary steps the tired pilgrims have to tread before they can reach the desired heaven. We must, as the Word teaches, take up the cross daily, not desiring to lay it down, but carry it faithfully to the end. How hard it is in youth and old age to have to carry the cross! But it seems the cross was made to carry,—no cross, no crown; and it is impossible that we could arrive at the beautiful garden of Paradise without first being acquainted with the garden of sorrow, where we have to pass through the different walks, and by the way would like to stoop down and pluck some beautiful flowers, almost forgetting that in sorrow's garden thorns and thistles only grow. No beautiful statues are there among the bitter plants; but the cross is there, and on it is written, "Remember, I have carried the cross before you, and follow in my footsteps."

This is the token of lowly Jesus. May we be meek and lowly as He was! And as He said of little children, "Suffer them to come unto me;" and also, in other words, "Except ye become as little children, ye shall in no wise enter the kingdom of heaven," may God help us all to realize what belongs to our peace, that we may be able to be called his chosen in life, in death, and through all eternity!

May the fiery trials which we have to pass through prove beneficial to us as we work out our own salvation; and the Holy Comforter that is sent to watch over us, and to lead and guide us, have occasion to say to each one of us, "This is my beloved child, in whom I am well pleased!" And may this be our watchword,—" God to glorify and humanity to bless and serve!" realizing that it is a delight to serve God, in fulfilling the command to love one another, and to have that "royal law" written in our hearts, that we be not like those that it speaks of in James, ii. 8, 15, 16, "If a brother or sister be naked, and destitute of daily food, and one of you say unto them, Depart in peace, be ye warmed and filled; notwithstanding ye give them not those things which are needful to the body; what doth it profit?" Even so, dear readers; our faith, if it has not works of this kind mentioned, is dead, being alone.

Let us closely examine these matters, and learn how necessary it is for us to serve God, through loving each other with a motherly love, and to feel that we minister a mother's love when we try to do all we can for each other in temporal and spiritual wants, as in Matthew, xxv., that those on the right hand, which are permitted to inherit the kingdom of heaven, are those "that have clothed the naked, given food to the hungry, drink to the thirsty, lodging to the stranger, and visited the sick and the imprisoned."

O thou Father, that beholdeth earth with thy all-seeing eye, watch over us poor, miserable sinners, that each and all may so live and act that we may hear that voice daily, "Good and faithful servant, enter thou into the joys of thy Lord."

Here Christ says that this welcome belongs to those that have performed all these things just mentioned; and to those on the left hand, that had not performed these loving deeds to the needy, "The King shall say unto them, Depart from me ye cursed." Then those on the left hand that could not come into the kingdom, said unto the Lord, "Lord, when saw we thee hungry, and gave thee no food; thirsty, and gave thee no drink; naked, and clothed thee not; sick, and visited thee not; in prison, and ministered not unto thee?" Then shall He answer them, "Verily I say unto you, Inasmuch as ye have not done it unto one of the least of these, ye did it not to me." "And these shall go away into everlasting punishment, but the righteous into life eternal."

If we reflect upon this in its true light, then we shall find that a love to the neighbor that has no sacrifice in it, nor any practical bearing, availeth nothing in the sight of God and his holy angels when they come to judge the world; because He says what we had done to one of the least of these, we had done it unto God.

Dear reader, let us meditate for a moment on the following remarks: If the Lord Jesus Christ should walk the earth to-day, as of old, the enlightened Christians and others would do anything to entertain Him. If He needed food, how many would try to be the first one that could have that worthy office to minister to Him! Food of the best kind that could ever be prepared would be offered unto Him; and, if he needed drink, likewise the finest and the most refreshing would be given to Him to allay his thirst with as He would be weary by the wayside. And if He needed lodging, how many would hasten to prepare the best guest-chamber for his reception! All this attention, because it was Jesus; and they would crowd in groups everywhere to see who would be the happy one to entertain Him, and to be honored with his presence. And if He was sick, oh, how they would watch over Him, night and day, with a mother's, brother's, and a sister's care, trying to be in his favor, because it was Jesus!

But oh, reader, stop right here with me, and, for the sake of our own salvation, let us consider what we are doing, and what are our thoughts on this subject! Let us not forget that we are to be judged according to the entertainments that we have bestowed on humanity's suffering ones, and that we are entertaining the Lord Jesus Christ when we entertain the suffering children of earth that stand in need of all these things, and are unable to procure the necessaries of life. Let us see to it in time, that we be not those on the left hand, that must depart because we have not given heed to those words that were spoken by the Lord while He was on the earth. This is what we must try to look into. Search the Scriptures on those points, as they have great bearing on our salvation.

Hoping that we may be able so to live and act, each one of us, that when the brother of low degree comes into our presence we may not scorn him because it is his lot to be poor, or because he has to work for his bread, having, perhaps, nothing but a morsel and a scanty lodging for all his toils, and frequently unable to obtain work to sustain life, while others roll in luxury and joy of every kind, unconcerned about the poor who, often for the want of proper employment fall into divers sins when all other sources fail for the sustenance of life; so they at last go down and downward until the grave receives the suffering body of destitution, and they leave a memory on earth of shame to themselves and others. Thus eternity has to witness the resurrection of fallen man; and, instead of joy among the angels in heaven over those that should be brought home to the fold, there is lamentation.

This is truth; no fiction! We are accountable, in a measure, for our neighbor's sins, in neglecting to study his welfare, and to do as Christ taught, "love one another as I have loved you." May God help us to fulfill the new command that Christ gave unto us, "to love one another;" and not like some, unwilling even to look upon our brother's miserable abode, his poor morsel, scanty clothing, and often the sick couch, without any one to give him a drop of water! But let us hasten, while there yet is time, to prepare to go to all these miserable abodes, to seek and rescue those which need our care and consolation; and in thus doing our duty we shall hear the loved voice of the Saviour say, "Come, ye blessed of my Father, inherit the kingdom prepared for you from the foundation of the world." Matt. xxv.

This is what will greet our ear, beloved fellow-traveler with me to the celestial city of peace, if we fulfill our blessed Master's command; and then in rapturous delight we shall sing and adore that God that loved us so that He sent his son into the world, that whosoever believed his sayings should have eternal life.

CHAPTER V.

*If we faithfully carry the cross,
We shall wear the crown;
If not willing to bear the cross,
We cannot wear the crown.*

WE find in the sacred words of Christ, that He said, "Be faithful unto death, and I will give to thee the crown of life." Now, this promise was only made to those that could faithfully carry out his sayings, and have such faith as He said we should have. May we get our understanding more enlightened regarding this faith that we ought to have in Christ, that we may comprehend more fully the new commandment that He gave unto us! This command includes more than faith. Heaven and earth bear witness to this command, and only as we are faithful to his teachings can we claim his promises.

Christ said, "Suffer little children to come unto me, and forbid them not, for of such is the kingdom of heaven." Let us examine this teaching, and see what it means; not baptism of infants, as some would suppose. No, it means just what He said in the following words: "Except ye become as little children, ye shall in no wise enter the kingdom of heaven." Let us commence, dear reader, to see what Christ commanded us to be, to fit us for the kingdom of heaven.

We have, first of all, to be spiritually born, —unfolded in wisdom and understanding,—so as to be acquainted with the laws of that kingdom that governs our inner being. It is necessary that we should look at our own standpoint, that we may be able to see where we stand, and to realize our need of a change of heart, and get a heart that will be free from sin and error, before we can become as little children, and be born of the spirit, which every one must be, before they can be fit subjects for that kingdom.

And, to enter into this new birth, we must, as St. Paul said, "bury the natural man, and die daily to self, to sin, to the lust of the eye, the pride of the flesh, and all that is vexatious to the spirit," and that can make it unfit to be born of the spirit of God; and to give up all that the natural man loves, with all the pleasures of this world's corruptive influence, and, instead, love all that is sublime and beautiful, and of a heavenly character, seeking only the glory of God,—which is to fulfill his command; and to have "that faith that worketh righteousness," remembering that Christ said "we shall be judged according to our works; and that each man's work shall be tried as with fire, that it may be seen of what sort it is."

May we all be able to lay more weight on the commands of Christ than upon a faith that has in it no substance of love! We must learn to know for ourselves, as another person could not be born of the spirit for you or me, any more than you could exist through another person's natural birth without being born a natural mortal yourself.

Now, this faith, preaching and believing, without its accompanying power of the holy spirit, the teacher that is to come and teach us in all things, cannot avail anything. When we have a desire to have our spiritual nature cultivated, that is, to love to have precious plants of a heavenly quality growing in our hearts, then the holy spirit—the spirit of truth—can find lodgment, and sow such seed as will produce fruit a hundred-fold.

It is impossible that this precious fruit can be produced while our hearts are in a condition not to receive any spiritual truth separate from a dead faith, which only teaches that Christ died, and did all for us. This faith is contrary to his teachings, and can only be called a delusion and an error, which will sink the whole human race deeper and deeper in ignorance, and forgetting the faith that Christ spoke of that we should have in Him, which was, that we should do the same works that

He did, and greater works than He did should we do (St. John, xiv. 12), because He went to the Father.

Now, He was born of this spirit, and He knew that we had to be like Him before we could be acquainted with the laws and liberties of that kingdom. Christ said it was necessary for Him to go; for if He did not go away, the Comforter could not come unto us. And He said, "If I depart, I will send Him unto you; and when He is come He will reprove the world of sin, ... because they believed not on me." "Of righteousness, because I go to my Father; and of judgment, because the Prince of this world is judged." John, xvi. 7–13. That is the evil of the natural man's unregenerated heart that is to be judged by this Comforter,—the spirit of truth,—that is sent to judge, teach, and guide into all truth.

It is necessary for us to commence to reflect in earnest, that we may see that we have something to do to regenerate our own hearts from sin and error, and not to think that all is done for us through Christ, and there is nothing to be done on our part only to live and be merry,—to speak and preach of this saving faith, which is only obtained by believing that Christ suffered to save us, and then we can enter into heaven.

Dear reader, where do we find the new birth,—the birth of the spirit,—in this dead faith? No, those who are born of the spirit of Christ live in the spirit. It has become their element; like the fish in the water, it lives and breathes only in its own atmosphere. So it is with us; when we become "new creatures" we live in the atmosphere of heaven's delight. All seems new to us. There is a new heaven and a new earth in the soul. Jesus knew that it had to be so,—a new creature of love to God and love to man; and old self must pass away, and the new-born creature must be guided by the spirit of truth. This is the "new birth,"—the seed of the word of truth that has taken root. It does not matter how it was ministered, or in what form it was received, if it was a living truth that fell in living ground. God prepared soil, that in spite of the enemy's sowing his tares, it will spring up and bear fruit; and, on account of its purity, will bear golden grain, fit for the harvest of the kingdom of heaven. Each one of us must be the reaper that brings in the good seed that has sprung up. After it has brought forth, we can feel the vibrating power of the love of God in the soul.

Let us see, dear reader, what the golden grain consists of. First, the seed of truth must be sowed in good ground. That is the heart prepared for the reception of the true seed; and to be willing to have a new heart changed into the delights of heaven, giving up all that has to be rooted up, which is sin and ignorance. Christ said, "Every plant which my heavenly Father has not planted, shall be rooted up." Matthew, xv. 13; and in St. John, xv. 2, we read, "Every branch in me that beareth not fruit He taketh away; and every branch that beareth fruit He purgeth it, that it may bring forth more fruit."

That shows us that it is only those plants that will bear fruit, or, in other words, can produce fruit, that our Father cares about spending any labor on, according to Christ's words.

All these plants referred to that must be pulled up by the roots, are the sins and iniquity of the human heart. A bad soil produces bad fruit. When the heart is in a fit state to receive the seed of the kingdom, then it will produce fruit; that as Christ said, "I am the vine, and ye are the branches. He that abideth in me, and I in him, the same bringeth forth much fruit." John, xv. 5. And then He says in verse 8, "Herein is my Father glorified, that ye bear much fruit." We learn by this that by a dead faith this fruit cannot be brought forth; but by living works. And in Malachi, iii. 10, "Bring ye all the tithes into the storehouse, that there may be meat in mine house, and prove me now herewith, said the Lord of hosts, if I will not open unto you the windows of heaven, and pour you out a blessing that there shall not be room enough to receive it."

My dear friends, we are to be co-laborers together in the great field of humanity; and that can only be brought about as we are first willing to set our own house in order before we commence with others. And when we feel the growth of this heavenly seed that has taken root in our heart, springing up and bearing fruit, then this glorious fruit is to feed others with; and our hearts are the garden that this fruit grew and ripened in. And as it drops its heavenly fruitage, the nations will eat and be satisfied, because it is truth. And so we will send out truth after truth, until the whole earth shall be filled with the glorious harvest of the kingdom which is to regenerate every human being. Yes, we must transplant from one to another, and thus see that the seed of truth can be sent abroad to every human soul, the life-giving seed of the kingdom.

And when this is sowed, it speaks of human love. Christ said, "As I have loved you, so you love one another." And, "as the Father has sent me, so I send you; and ye abide in my love." Now, we learn by this, that we are commanded to have the same intense love for each other that He had, and then to go with this message He was sent to bear. He was the living, practical example in whose mouth was no guile. We cannot possibly say we do not know how to follow Him, because we read through the blessed record that He tells us to "search the Scriptures," to learn how to fulfill his Father's will. He said He was sent for that purpose. He never said He sent Himself, but that He was sent to show us the way and how to walk in his footsteps.

Let us not think that that human love which He practiced in his exemplary life ceased there with the finishing of his mission. No, far from that; but on account of misunderstanding his mission, the world is becoming worse, because many think they had Christ to do all for them in fulfilling his mission, and think that they have no duties to perform either to God or man. The most advisable thing we can do is to commence in earnest to lay hold on the things belonging to our salvation, and remember the words written in Phil. ii. 12, that we have to work out our own salvation with fear and trembling, and begin to realize that we are placed here on earth as accountable beings. It is impossible to be followers of Christ without having responsibilities; for there is a responsibility in the very command —" Take up the cross and follow Him daily."

Thus fulfilling your duty faithfully; and, instead of being those servants who thought they had Christ to do all for them and taken their sins upon Him, they still continuing in their sins; so that whatever they did, it was an Almighty atoner that suffered for their transgressions. Christ never introduced such a doctrine. He said, " If ye love me, keep my commandments. He it is that loveth me that keepeth my sayings."

Jesus said, "If a man love me he will keep my words; and my Father will love him, and we will come unto him. And he that loveth me not, keepeth not my sayings; and the word which ye hear is not mine, but the Father's, which sendeth me." John, xiv. 23, 24.

May God show us our duties, that we may be able to see the King in his beauty, and be like a holy army that has set out for the holy city of peace, whose portals those inhabitants have entered, that followed the Master wheresoever he went! May the great King enlighten each one how to find the holy city,— the New Jerusalem that is coming down from heaven as a bride adorned for the bridegroom! And may the peace of that holy city, whose builder and maker is God, overshadow us with the holy spirit, that we may get our understanding enlightened, and behold the King in his glory, as he descends with his holy angels, teaching us lessons of redeeming love!

CHAPTER VI.

My cross I will carry, though foes me beset,
The crown I shall gain if faithful I can prove;
Then in rapturous delight with angels bright
We shall hail each weary pilgrim
That their crosses hath laid down,
And exchanged them for the immortal crown.

    This crown is for those
    That the hungry have fed
    And the naked have clothed;
    That have visited the sick,
    And the stranger lodged,
    And ministered to the prisoners
    Love's comforting words.

    Showing forth to the world
    That Christ in his commands
    Bids us go to the lowly, the
    Forsaken, and to sinners
    He called; and only as we
    Like Him will be to the prisoner's
    Cell, and the afflicted, we will go.

    That the religion of Christ
    May be felt on the earth,
    That whatever we do
    To one of the least of these,
    We do it unto God.

Of those elements the wedding garment must be made. The pure and undefiled religion must be practiced amongst the mortals of earth, which is "to visit the fatherless and the widow in their affliction, and to keep ourselves unspotted from the world."

That we may not be like the five foolish virgins, which we read of in Matth. xxv., that had not prepared oil in their lamps, and expected to meet the bridegroom. "And at night there was a cry made, Behold, the bridegroom cometh; go ye out to meet him." And the five wise virgins had their lamps trimmed, and burning with divine love, and were ready to meet the bridegroom, and to go in unto the marriage. And the door was shut. But the five foolish had to tarry behind, because their lamps would not burn, on account of not having any oil. So they had to go and buy oil; and after they also came, and wanted to come in, and said, "Lord, open unto us." But He said, "Verily I say unto you, I know you not." And they could not come into the marriage supper. Read Matt. xxv. Here we have the two representatives of the ten virgins. The five foolish are those that have faith, but do not follow his commands; and the five wise, that prepared for his coming, are they that have faith with works.

Again, we read in Matt. xxii. 11, "When the king came in to see the guests that were assembled at the marriage feast, he saw there a man which had not on a wedding garment; and he said unto him, Friend, how comest thou in hither, not having a wedding garment? And he was speechless from surprise at these words of the king; and it was commanded to take him out and cast him into utter darkness."

Let us take in consideration that we cannot, according to God's Word, enter heaven without having on the wedding garment. Some would say to this, How are we to prepare for it? By fulfilling what we have already written, —to be able to love others as ourselves; not thinking that we can have the garment of sin, scorn, selfishness, and yet enter in through the door that leadeth into the marriage supper. No, we must abandon sin and selfishness, as they are hinderances.

We must first put away all unrighteousness, and make our hearts a marriage altar, where we desire to live unto God and the neighbor; to be pure and holy in heart, and to feel that Christ and the holy angels help us if we are willing to prepare for this. He has said, "No one can come unto the Father but through me." "I am the door." Now, to be initiated into "the heavenly marriage," and have Christ for our bridegroom, it is necessary, to be a complete marriage, that there should be unity. The natural marriage is never complete without harmony and unity. Then, first, it is a foretaste of heaven on earth. And so it is with our unity in Christ,—we must be in unity with Him in all that pertains to his sacrificing love to be his bride.

He said, "Seek me while ye can find me."

"I am the light of the world." And if we do his will He and the Father will come and take up their abode in our hearts. May God help us all to realize the true state we have to be in! For, to have the Father and the Son take up their abode with us, the heart must certainly be a fit temple for the Holy Spirit,— the spirit of peace and wisdom, that will lead us in all things.

Now, we cannot serve two masters at one time. We must give up the one and serve the other,—God or Mammon,—whichever we will choose. And if we will serve God, we must fulfill his command, in doing as we are taught, through Christ's teaching.. We cannot possibly please God, or have a clear conscience, unless we observe that which He wishes us to do. Christ said, "Ye are my disciples if ye do whatsoever ye are commanded to do for each other." And He teaches us, in Matt. vii. 12, "Therefore all things whatsoever ye would that men should do to you, do ye even so to them: for this is the law and the prophets." "And to fulfill the whole law which is fulfilled in one word, thou shalt love thy neighbor as thyself." Gal. v. 14. This is the law and the testimony that Christ gave unto us. Search the Scripture for these things, and we shall gain light to our understanding.

We need a religion of love,—not to serve God only by church-going, but in human acts of love, kindness, and fellowship in all that pertains to their earthly interest and salvation. We are to be saved by a faith that worketh love and charity to humanity's suffering ones. Let us remember, Christ has taught us, through his sacrificing life, that we must follow in his footsteps; and as the body without the spirit is dead, so is faith without works dead also. James, ii. Oh, let us give more earnest heed to those things, in order to commence to be practical Christians, and fulfill his teachings, and live out "the royal law," according to the Scriptures, "in loving our neighbor as ourselves;" and as we strive to be citizens of heaven, may we learn that we must, while on earth, live under its law, which is love!

Heaven is full of love; and multitudes of earth pray daily that God's will may be done on earth as it is in heaven. So we must fulfill "this royal law;" for that is the law of heaven, and of its Christ.

May God open our understanding, that we may understand the Scripture! This we are to pray for, that we may not walk in a faith without light, but may realize that Christ was that light that came and showed us the way, through his teachings of redeeming love; and as we read in Romans, viii. 9, 10, that "if any man have not the spirit of Christ, he is none of his." And only as we can be like Him can we expect to be united with Him, and have Him come and take up his abode in our hearts, and thus become the center of our affection.

May we be able to realize what belongs to

our peace, and that we are here "to work out our own salvation;" and it must be after the pattern of Christ as regards human love and sacrifice! May the spirit of truth remain with us, and teach us how to purge sin and corruption from our hearts, that we may abide solely in the teachings of the Master, that we may be benefited unto salvation, remembering that the Word teaches "that we are to pay to the uttermost farthing in all we do!"

How necessary, then, it is to watch over ourselves, not forgetting that we are accountable beings! May the great God help us to be on our guard, and remember to look to Him in all our times of need; and be able to have the whole armor on when we are to fight for the truth as it is in the Lord Jesus Christ, so as to enter without spot or blemish, having our garments pure and undefiled, and be the virgins that have the lamps filled with oil, so that if we are called at any time, morning, noon, or night, we will be ready to hear the bridegroom's voice, "Enter, ye blessed, into the kingdom of my Father!"

Now, it is necessary so to live that we can have heaven within; and if we have heaven within while we live, we must surely have that which pertains to the Father, the Son, and the holy angels. This is what we must be conscious of in our hearts; and to realize that God's laws are written there. Heb. viii. 10. And we shall then be able to walk in his statute. This must be the state of things to have the kingdom of heaven within. We cannot possibly know what it is to live with this heavenly kingdom in our hearts, or enter there after death, except we be acquainted with that kingdom, its inhabitants, its language, and its laws. We must be citizens of that kingdom by following out its laws while we live here on earth.

May God, in his mercy, show us how to live, so that his laws can be written in our hearts,—his will be done on earth as it is done in heaven! That is, if we make up our minds to live Christ's life, we must realize that we are to blend with the spirit of Christ and the holy angels as they come to minister unto us. They have heaven in their hearts, and teach us in their sacred mission to die daily unto sin and put on Christ. And may we remember, no one "can see God without purity and holiness;" and He has ordained all for our temporal and spiritual wants, that we may be able to serve Him in spirit and in truth, if we are minded to study our eternal interest!

Let us that do not yet fully realize the means sent to us for salvation, look to this more earnestly, and study the holy Scripture in a prayerful spirit, that we may get our understanding enlightened on these points, and realize, that if we desire to worship God in spirit and in truth, we shall be led and guided by that holy ministration that is sent through his holy angels, leading us in the road we are to go to find the holy city of peace.

May we be the ones that enter in through

the door, which is Christ, not trying to climb over the fence some other way; but feeling that Christ is that way, and that we must be prepared to follow in his steps, and have Him for our constant pattern; not to be like the man who thought he could be admitted as a wedding guest, but found, when he came in there, that he did not have on the wedding garment, and could not belong to that company, but rather like those we read of in Revelation, vii. 14, "That had come out of great tribulations, purified their garments, and made them white in the blood of the Lamb," which is to be in unity with Christ and his sufferings and sacrifices of human love! No completeness without unity; we must be in that unity to be followers of Christ. This man did not know what it was to be a follower of Christ; and he could not remain with those that belonged to that heavenly marriage company. Had he heeded Christ's voice, He would have known him, and all would have been well with him. Christ said He was the shepherd, and "my sheep hear my voice, and follow me." But this man listened not to the voice of our heavenly shepherd; he did not know Christ, and had not adopted his teachings.

How many, Christ said, should seek the way and not find it! And how many are called, but how few are chosen, because they are not willing to carry their crosses, and walk in the way that Christ pointed out for them, in taking up the cross daily and following Him!

O God, the Father, Son, and Holy Spirit, help us to find the way that leadeth in through the straight gate to the celestial city, that we may be able to see the King in his beauty, and open the door of our hearts, that He can enter and take up his abode there, and shed abroad the heavenly marriage delights! May we be able so to listen to his teachings that we can say that we live daily within the sanctuary of Christ, which is to blend in unison with his heart, to which the whole heavens pulsate in rapport,—till we become so enrapt in Him, and all that belongs to the fold of the Father, that the whole heaven encircles us daily; feeling that it is delightful to serve God and do his will, in living for humanity, as Christ did, and so fulfill that faith that He said we should have, which was, that we should do the same works as He did, and greater works should we do than He did, because He had to go to the Father! That shows us that we were left to finish that which He commenced. " He finished his work," and by his example showed us that we had not to stop there; but that we were to go on, as He said, " Be ye perfect, even as your Father which is in heaven is perfect." Matt. v. 48.

Great God, help us to lean more upon the teachings of the Bible! to investigate its precious truth,—not to be satisfied with a creed made by men, claiming a few sentiments only of the Bible as basis of their creed, and the rest is thought contrary to Christ's teachings; and let us seek for ourselves, as Christ said, " Search the Scriptures; they shall testify of me." In observing the sayings of Christ, it gives us the privilege to grow in wisdom and understanding, and not to be narrowed down to some man's mind of the past or present, that formed creeds according to his standard of religious views of that time; but may we realize that we must be born anew of the spirit, and that there is a fruit of this spiritual birth! When we are born anew of the spirit of God, we shall then be like, as Christ declares, "a tree that beareth good fruit a hundred-fold." This is, as the Word teaches in Luke, viii., Matt. vii., St. John, xv., the good seed that was sown in good ground, and sprang up and bore fruit to the glory of God. And, as Christ said, "In this is my Father glorified, that ye bear much fruit." When we have such offerings to present to our heavenly Father, then first can we realize that we are the chosen disciples that follow Christ faithfully, being, as we read in Phil. i. 11, "filled with the fruits of righteousness, which are by Jesus Christ unto the glory and praise of

God." And in Acts, x. 34, 35, "That God is no respecter of persons; but in every nation he that feareth Him, and worketh righteousness, is accepted with Him." "For hereunto were ye called, because Christ also suffered for us, leaving us an example, that ye should follow his steps." I. Peter, ii. 21.

May we all in time get the eyes of our spiritual understanding open, that we may understand the Scripture, so as to be able to realize that we have something to do besides believing, in order to be saved; not to read the Bible merely as a history of Christ, thinking by so doing that we have gained salvation, forgetting ourselves that we have a charge to keep, as we read in Phil. ii. 12, "to work out our own salvation with fear and trembling," after the pattern of Christ.

Let us search the Scripture in earnest for these things, and we shall find that almost on every page it points us to a crucified Saviour, who wishes us to adopt his teachings of humiliation, love, and forbearance; and even shows us, in his dying hours of agonizing suffering, that He was not in the least changed, but patiently endured in his human kindness and affection to the last, when He whispered forth in his dying moments, "Father, forgive them, for they know not what they do." Thus we have much to learn before we can be like that suffering Lamb. We find in his teachings (John, vii. 17), that "if any man will do God's will, he shall know of the doctrine;" and that "He would pray for us," under the peculiar trials which we have to pass through, "that our faith should not fail."

He knew, when He uttered those last words of forgiveness for his enemies, that his earthly mission was drawing near to a close. If we reflect on that perfect example of human love and human suffering, we can understand that his whole life, from the beginning of his calling, was a life in obedience to his Father's will. He said, "I come not to do my own will, but the will of Him that sent me." John, vi. 38; and in xii. 26, "If any man serve me, let him follow me; and where I am, there shall also my servant be; and him will my Father honor." "And as I come to fulfill my Father's will, so ye fulfill my commands in loving each other as I have loved you."

Now, this was the teaching of Jesus eighteen hundred and seventy-one years ago, while He was on earth; and the same seemed to be his teaching after his death, on many occasions, when He appeared to his disciples. John, xx. 17, 21. The first person He appeared to was Mary, and requested her to go and say to his brethren, "I ascend unto my Father, and your Father; and to my God, and your God;" and the same day He appeared to his disciples, and said, "Peace be unto you! As the Father hath sent me, even so I send you." So it seemed it was his only desire that we should fulfill our mission, as he had fulfilled his, He being the perfect example for us to go by.

Now, if his teachings had been followed up since that time, and if the people had been in a state to live a life of such sacrifice and human love as He commanded, and which He set forth through his exemplary life, there would be a different state of things at present in the world and in the professed church of Christ. The whole world would be a glorious church of Christ, where love and charity would beam forth everywhere in loving deeds of sympathy and compassion for the afflicted, the destitute, the oppressed, and the downtrodden. Thus our religion would be to do unto others as to ourselves, for our neighbor's needs, both spiritual and temporal, are the same as our own. Christ was that church, and through his exemplary life He showed us the interior of that church; so if we love to serve and worship in that church, we have to adopt his teachings, and follow in his steps daily. Then we worship our heavenly Father in spirit and in truth, as Christ did, He being the mediator of the new covenant between God and man.

But, instead of this heavenly law of love

lived out to each other, faith only in the Son of God has become prevalent on the earth, without that practical teaching that He showed forth in his life, and set forth in his doctrine. Now, " He being the brightness of his glory, and the express image of his person, by his example He teaches us how we are to live pure and holy. He was full of charity and love for the oppressed, lifting the sinner that lay at his feet, saying, He did not condemn her, but bade her go and sin no more.

It is time that we commence to adopt his precepts of love and compassion to those that need our spiritual and temporal care, not thinking that we can be perfect followers of the Master before we be imbued with the same love that He had in his heart for the oppressed and down-trodden.

Let us reflect upon this in its true light, as it is one of the most important subjects which belong to us as reformers of the fallen human race.

We will commence by saying, Begin to

prepare to meet the Bridegroom. He may call you in the night-watch to blend with his heart of loving compassion for this unfortunate class of both sexes; and, oh! will you then say to Him, Wait till a more convenient season, and I will call for thee? Then, perhaps, it will be too late, and He whom you profess to follow has returned to those that are the chosen ones. The Word teaches many are called but few chosen. Let us strive to be the chosen ones that hear this midnight cry of the Bridegroom, and feel that we are to blend with the heavenly and the divine; and as we are called on this sacred mission, let us summon the people together, as a midnight cry, to redeem the forlorn and destitute, who then flock from their dens of intoxication and houses of infamy. But stay,—let us reflect on this "midnight call." Who has a sister, a brother, a child on this road that leadeth to destruction, and in the silent hour of midnight is seeking to find some victim of either sex, that they may entice to their miserable abode?

Oh, *ye* MINISTERS OF THE GOSPEL! *ye* that are *the leaders* of the *flock! to you, to one and all*, is this midnight call. Hear ye what the Saviour has said: "If ye love me keep my commandments, and teach men to do likewise," not in words only. Christ said, "Not every one that saith unto me, Lord, Lord, shall enter into the kingdom of heaven, but he that doeth the will of my Father which is in heaven." Let us closely examine this saying. It does not consist in preaching and hearing only, but in unwavering faith with practical works. Now, "faith without works is dead, being alone." So, then, if faith without works is dead, we must be up and doing; calling together the lost sheep, even though it should be at the midnight-watch.

Oh, may all who profess to be *living* followers of Christ be able to hear the Shepherd's voice, speaking to us as He did to Peter, "Lovest thou me?" then "Feed my sheep!" The question was again repeated, Peter responding, "Thou knowest all things. Thou knowest that I love thee." To which the Lord answered, "Feed my sheep, feed my lambs." And when He had spoken this, He saith unto him, "Follow me." Let us follow this teaching of Peter, and not imitate his example when, at the midnight cock-crowing, he denied his Lord, saying, "I know not the man."

Help us, O Lord, to realize what is required of us as professing Christians and followers of the Lamb of God! O thou great Shepherd and King of heaven and of earth, in whose hand is the scepter of power to rule all things, we pray thee to have patience with all the Peters who are not willing to take up the cross and follow Thee, if necessary, to the garden of Gethsemane, in prayer for the sin and destruction that covers this earth.

O God, help us, or we perish in the midst of the harvest, and our lambs shall lack pasture!

May we be able to lead them to living

streams of purity and delight, where their weary and sinking spirit shall find repose on the bosom of some loving mother or sister, who will shelter those forlorn and destitute in their homes!

Mothers, husbands, brothers, and sisters, rescue the forlorn, the forsaken, that have none to shed the tear of sympathy over their fallen condition, or to hear their desolate anguish, no one who cares for them, no one who heeds the Saviour's warning voice, "Feed my sheep." Oh, sisters and brothers in the Lord, be swift in your doings, for the Lord cometh as a thief in the night, and who shall be ready to appear? He calls you to prepare for the battle, for the great day of his wrath is come, and you cannot stand and meet the Bridegroom without the bridal robes. Ye are my beloved if ye do whatsoever I have commanded you. "I go to prepare a place for you, that where I am ye may be also."

Follow me in the night-watches, follow me in the garden of sorrow, follow me in prayer and love,—a bright crown shall adorn the brow of the faithful child that follows me. Oh, sleep not, watcher, but prepare for the sudden changes that shall come. Who shall be the virgins that shall be found wanting oil for their lamps? Buy while it is day, that when the night cometh ye may be able to meet the Bridegroom and hear his voice. He speaks to you in tender tones. Follow me to the garden of Paradise, where is the river of life, and in the midst the tree of knowledge, and its leaves are for the healing of the nations.

Oh, take this healing balm, and carry it to every troubled breast. Tell them of the land of pure delight, where the weary and repentant child of earth shall be at rest for evermore.

And let us, in prayer and thanksgiving, feel that it is a privilege to be commissioned to follow in the footsteps of the Master. May we be so enrapt in the redemption of fallen humanity that our highest desire shall be to live for them as Christ did, and bring to them the nectar of prayer, that they may drink and feel it is a sweet balm, and a safeguard to their souls, to observe that which Christ taught, namely, to "Watch and pray, lest ye fall into temptation;" and the day of God's grace will pass, and you will sink deeper and deeper into degradation and vice, till you are past redemption, and must belong to those that we read of in the Word,—the deceiver, the liar, and the adulterer. They are the ones that cannot enter the kingdom of heaven. May your hearts daily be lifted up to God, praying for guidance; and may we all be in a pure and holy state, and the holy angels that are sent to guard us on our pilgrimage, find our life blending with theirs in heavenly purity; and instead of making victims of sin, may we try to rescue them from error, helping them to tread in the path of purity and virtue, remembering that it is our sisters and brothers of humanity, and that we only do our duty as we would that others should do unto us and our dear ones, were they in the road of temptation, sin, and error!

A word of advice. Pilgrims on life's journey,—you that profess to be followers of meek and lowly Jesus, and place yourselves, through the membership of some church, as an example to the world,—see to it, that you may not, through the example of your life, be a stumbling-block of shame and offense to the world, and be forced to hear this of yourselves and your professed brethren, as we often have to hear, "If this or that one is a church-member, then I do not want to be one!"

Let us be the ones that, through the membership of the church, shall be examples of the Master to the world, that all may flock to us, desiring to learn of the teachings, that they also may be like unto ourselves. And thus we shall go hand-in-hand on the pilgrimage of life, walking in the road that leadeth heavenward, and letting nothing be lost by the wayside; but gathering up the broken sheaves and binding their wounds of sin and shame, by pouring the oil of heavenly joys into their souls, leading them as with a true mother's care, that they may be inmates of the heavenly city. We shall then, while we are on life's pilgrimage, cause joy among the angels in heaven over sinners that have repented. And thus we shall go on, and on, being blessed daily, and blessing others, by the purity of our lives.

This is to observe the teachings of Jesus, and to learn of Him how to become pure and holy, so as to be able to follow his precepts. And when the weary traveler is through with the pilgrimage of earth, we shall stand arrayed in the loveliness of Christ, for we have conquered unto salvation; and the fallen and destitute that we found by the wayside, or in some lonely hut of suffering, has been benefited by the teachings of Christ's love, fulfilled in us, and made practical to each other. And in so doing, we can be the ones that are saved by faith, because we have believed in the teachings of Christ, and been the sheep that knew his voice and followed Him daily.

Now, if we have not Jesus that walks the earth to-day, as of old, we have that blessed assurance that He has been on the earth, to teach us how to live, that we may reach heaven. He knew what it was to be a true cross-bearer; and He still sympathizes with us as we carry our crosses, if we are willing to come to terms with the saving means which is to work out our own salvation after the pattern of Christ's humiliation, love, forbearance, charity, purity; feeling, if we have not Jesus' feet to lay down at, we have the foot of the cross, that He has told us to carry daily, if we love to follow Him.

Beloved reader, we are, then, very near his feet, if we follow close in his footsteps. And further, He directs us to sell our riches, if we have any, "and give unto the poor," and so keep the commandments,—the two greatest, the first of which is "to love God with all our heart, soul, and mind,"—that is, in thanking

Him for all we have; in doing his will,—and the second is like unto it, "to love the neighbor as ourselves. On these two commandments hang all the law and the prophets."

And the new commandment,—the eleventh in order which He gave unto us,—"that we should love one another as He has loved us." John, xiii. 34. "Love worketh no ill to his neighbor; therefore love is the fulfilling of the law," as we read in Romans, xiii. 10; Gal. v. 14, "For all the law is fulfilled in one word, even in this: Thou shalt love thy neighbor as thyself;" and in II. John, ix., "Whosoever transgresseth, and abideth not in the doctrine of Christ, hath not God. He that abideth in the doctrine of Christ, he hath both the Father and the Son."

Dear reader, it is impossible to become an heir of the kingdom of heaven without this love in the heart; for we must love and promote each other's happiness, and become like little children in love, remembering that of such innocence and purity is the kingdom of heaven. We must be willing to be taught lessons of the redeeming love ; and after we realize that we have undergone daily purification in our hearts, we must think of our poor brother that travels with us on life's pilgrimage to the city of peace,—to rescue him as he walks on the road that leads him away from the heavenly city.

May we realize, in extending the hand of help to our brother, that we can be the means of rescuing him from error and wrongs, and remember that we are only sojourners here on earth for a time, and that this is not our abiding place; and may we be able so to live while we are on this life's pilgrimage, as though we were like travelers who have set out for the celestial city,—the New Jerusalem, —and do all for each other that we possibly can! If any are naked, give them clothing ; hungry, feed them ; and, if able to work, incite them to industry, and advance their interest ; and, if not understanding, but willing, to work, teach them, and cultivate their genius and their minds, that they may fulfill the place in society that our heavenly Father intended they should have.

And do as you would to your own dear ones, were they without work, or bread, or opportunities for a proper training of their faculties, and let the light of Christ's love shine forth daily in living acts, so that you belong not to the class we read of in James, ii., that could not profit by faith only. It reads thus: "If a brother or sister be naked, and destitute of daily food, and one of you say to them, Depart in peace, be ye warmed and filled; notwithstanding ye give him not those things which are needful to the body; what doth it profit? Even so faith, if it hath not works, is dead, being alone."

Let us take the writings of the Bible into consideration, and be willing to help each other while we are on the pilgrimage of earth; that we may be the good Samaritan, that had all possible concern for his fellow-brethren, and did all for them that they needed in the time of want. And if we ourselves should be unable to procure comforts for the suffering and destitute ones that come under our observation, let us call upon the rich, that have of this world's goods, and have them lend a helping hand, from love and charity to the neighbor; remembering, if we give all, and have not charity, which is love in the heart for the neighbor, it availeth nothing to the giver,—only benefiting the one that receives it. So let us perform all noble deeds from a loving heart, remembering, when we go on our missions of love, that Christ taught us how to love each other! Thus observing and performing deeds of charity, we make ourselves friends of the angels, who never become weary in going with us on such holy missions. And when it sometimes seems as though we should faint through discouragement, to see this world of sin and the lack of Christ's love in their hearts, then we are surrounded by their presence; and our heavenly Father has said, "They shall hold us up in all our ways," and wrap their mantle of love and strength about us.

O God, help us to realize our mission of love to each other on the earth, and as we go to the rich man in behalf of the poor, may we be able to touch some chord of human sympathy and benevolence in his heart for the oppressed and afflicted; and then, as he passed by some miserable dwelling where a child of sorrow and deprivation dwelt which needed help and consolation, his heart would be glowing with the love of Christ for the needy, because that chord of sweet charity, which is love, has been touched with the divine flame of God's love.

I say again, in pleading for the poor to the rich, after first having done all we can ourselves for the relief of the needy, we not only derive benefit and eternal happiness to ourselves, but we cause eternal happiness to the rich man, that his portion may not be like the one that Christ spoke of,—the rich man and Lazarus in eternity.

Oh, children of earth, rich and poor, I beg of you to commence preparing your wedding garments for eternity! They must be made of human deeds of kindness, benevolence, and heavenly love. You must be prepared to receive the *One—our* beloved Christ—that performed like deeds, and be baptized with the same baptism as He was baptized with, and drink of the same cup as He drank of. He declares, through the Word, that is what is necessary, if you want to enter heaven.

Christ spake through a parable, and said that "the kingdom of heaven is likened unto a leaven, which a woman took and hid in three measures of meal." Let us, too, commence in earnest to lay hold of this leaven, and work so that the whole may be leavened; and let us not give ourselves any peace until we are sure we have found the road that leadeth to the celestial city, even if we have to carry innumerable crosses with us, and help others also to carry theirs; remembering that we are to carry each other's burdens, and so fulfill the love of Christ!

May sinners be converted through the purity, and loveliness, and efforts of your lives, as set forth in your daily walks; and may a living religion, that speaks in living representations of Christ, be the mirror into which they can look to find those followers of the Saviour's love! And if we have a mite or two, or more, let us not be slow to assist our fellow-travelers, who travel with us on life's pilgrimage, or whatever we can bestow upon them, that we may not belong to those that crowd the temples of earth which are made with hands, regardless of following in the Master's footsteps, forgetting that we are to assemble ourselves to worship in spirit and in truth that God who dwells in temples not made with human hands, eternal in the heavens. May God help us, or we perish! and we be at last like that servant who had not on the wedding garment!

But may we, instead, be like the servant that did his Father's will, took up his cross daily, and followed Christ faithfully unto the end, remembering the promise of Christ, to be "faithful unto death, and I will give thee the crown of life!"

THE CROSS.

THE cross of Christ is heavy to carry,
And many fall beneath its weight;
But Jesus taught you how to carry it,
That you may not sink beneath its weight.

He taught you to follow in his steps,
And He your guide should be,
Through the lessons sublime that He left,—
They shall teach of his love to thee.

And when the crosses of earth you have carried,
Then you shall find in rapturous delight,
That God loved you so that He sacrificed
His Son, to teach you how to find rest
In yon heaven with Christ for evermore.

Pilgrims of the cross of Christ,
He invites you to follow in his steps;
And speaks to you inviting words
Of happiness and peace for evermore.

A peace that the weary traveler needs,—
A rest which the weary traveler seeks,—

He gives it, if you follow in his steps.
He is the Way, the Truth, the Light sublime.

Thus you must follow the Master divine,—
Not to lay down the burden before its time;
And then you will find the lessons sublime
When you arrive at that beautiful home
Where blossoms perfume and odor the whole.

Then the weary pilgrim has found his rest;
No more sorrow, no more death.
And Jesus watches to see how many
His sublime teachings like to follow.
Such He invites, and makes them be at peace,—
Free forever from Oppression's heavy yoke.

THE CROSS-BEARER.

THE cross of Christ is heavy to carry,
But the Christian does not its burden feel;
They shrink for awhile, but soon its beauty
They shall perceive.

Of thorns and thistles the crosses are made,—
They come from Sorrow's tree;
Blossoms do not grow on Sorrow's tree,
Still the foliage is as green.

Immortelles is the name of the flowers
That lie hidden underneath this cross;
And the Christian carries it in the hope
That their beauty will be seen.

So the beauty of the cross of Christ
Has no beauty to the eye;
But, oh! wanderer of earth,
Its beauty you can only see
As you follow in his steps.

And thus Christians travel on
Until we reach our heavenly home,
Where all shall be so delightful,
For Jesus is there to welcome us home.

There in that beautiful home of God
We shall find many that loved us on earth,
Ready and willing to hear our wish,
And with us live and reign in heavenly bliss.

THE CROWN.

DEAR pilgrim on life's journey, crosses
Of every size and hue you must carry;
But remember, no cross, no crown,
Awaits the child that has not followed Christ.

In those steps commences
The Christian's pilgrimage of earth;
Weary and forsaken, traveling with sadness,
Christ says, " Be faithful unto death,
And I will give thee the crown of life.

Immortality is its name;
Of sorrow and earth's thistles was it made;
Many tears, many blasted hopes,
Many of life's bitter vicissitudes
Compose the beauty of this crown
Of peace, happiness, and rest for evermore.

Thus earth's weary pilgrim must struggle
To bear the cross and win the crown.
Jesus whispers, " Be faithful unto death,
And I will bless thy weary steps.

" And as you carry it in hope and faith,
Following my weary steps,
I shall be with thee, weary one of earth.
I see all your sorrows, I see all your tears,—
Bright jewels they will be in the crown for thee."

And when the sorrows of earth are past,
The cross will be changed into a crown of gold.
If, while on earth, crosses with Christ you have changed,
Then the weariness will be ended forever;
For there, in the mansions of the blest,
Will be no more sorrow,—no more death.

THE PALM OF VICTORY.

REST not, weary pilgrim, till the palm
Of victory you have gained.
Sorrow's banner shields thee on earth,
That the glorious victory you cannot see;
But the faithful soldier of the cross
Must fight for the kingdom of his God

Till his mission is ended here below.
Then he shall find the palm of victory
Will crown him on eternity's morn.
It will be the emblem to show that he
Has conquered unto salvation; and the
Helmet shall be adorned with laurels of victory.

Thus the faithful soldiers of the Lord
That have come out of the warfare of
Tribulation, shall be arrayed in the crown
And the palm, as a sign that they
Have fought well under the banner of love
While on earth,—conquering the evils
Of the natural man, and put on Christ
As the breastplate of righteousness.

THE WEDDING GARMENT.

SOLDIER of the cross of Christ, see that you are attired in the full heroic suit that belongs to the true cross-bearer, that intends to join the marriage company of heaven.

>Purity, charity, and love to God and man,
>Is the name of the attire you must have on

to be counted worthy to be a wedding guest of the household of the redeemed. And, as you are welcome there, see that you have on the garment of Christ's love, which will show you are a faithful cross-bearer of his cross, and that you may hear jubilee sung over the faithful soldier that has come home. Then the kingdom is won, because we accepted God's laws, and his will, to come in our hearts while on earth.

And we can then sing with Jesus, "Father, the cup is past, and the glory of thy kingdom is come for ever and ever!" And the angels that were sent to comfort, guard, and teach us, will sit together with us, praising God for every faithful soldier that has come home to his Father's house, laid down his cross, and is attired in the wedding garment, the palm of victory, and the crown of immortality.

THE CELESTIAL CITY.

THUS the soldier, being arrayed in the wedding garment, is a fit wedding guest for the king to behold. Let us faithfully see to it, that we may be able to be counted worthy to belong to that heavenly marriage company that have found the way into the holy city whose builder and maker is God. And may we feel that we must have the whole attire on before we can be called a faithful crossbearer,—one in whom God is well pleased!

And when we arrive, my dear reader, into this glorious New Jerusalem,—the holy city of our God,—we can then sit down in the rest of heaven's delight, relating to each other the story of our crosses of earth. And, as I shall relate it there, when, in unison with the cross-bearers that have become angels, I will now close my story of the Changed Cross by saying to you, my reader,—

> There was once a cross I loved to carry,
> Flowers of earth were its name;
> But soon its beauty faded away,
> And, methought, a new one I must make.
>
> So, one after another, its beauties I learned to see
> Fade before my sight, till at last, behold! no

Flower could I find that on my cross would
Stay; but each seemed to whisper sadness
In its fragrance and decay.

Then came to me one that became to my heart
So dear. He said, Change crosses with me, my child;
I have carried this for many a year,
And know its weight you would not feel.
It is not adorned with flowers; its beauty
Withered before the morning dew.

The one I offer you is wet with Sorrow's dew,—
Many tears, many blasted hopes, many
That have put thorns on its bosom instead of flowers.
Mine is a perpetual solitude, and on its surface
You will see written, Sorrow lasted but for
A day; but sunshine cometh on the morrow.

So we must be courageous, willing, and enduring,— not grieving for unseen to-morrow. The storms rage. How necessary, you see, it is to hold fast to the cross that the Saviour offers, as the anchor of our hopes! And He only knows that you must be willing to carry it all alone. He said, "Trust me, and I will be your guide, till you reach that home where sorrow, sickness, and trials are never known." Then, instead, we shall have our Father's smiles, that will chase our gloom away; and, in the tranquil hour, when the laborer's work of life is done, then in heavenly serenity he shall find the shining river; and beyond its waters shall appear the celestial mansion.

> Oh, there is waiting a mansion rare,—a city in the sky,
> Where the inhabitants are of one accord;
> They enchant the regions of their celestial abode!
> Oh, there are no thorns or hardened roads
> To walk upon as messengers from their God!
>
> They hasten therefrom with human love,
> Their bosoms filled with love divine.
> And thus they fulfill their Father's will,
> Those angels of the celestial court;
> And to many a sorrowful heart they come,
> Pouring oil of gladness in their soul,
> That speaks of a heaven after the crosses are past,
> Where they will have no more crosses to carry.

They bid us prepare to inhabit those places heaven has in store for every weary child that carries the cross faithfully to the end and obeys the Saviour's command, through those that were sent to testify of his love. He says, Follow me on, until you reach the summit of perfection, where all the heavy crosses of the earth shall shine in resplendent beauty. If we had carried no cross on earth, we could not be counted among those that had come out of great tribulation, and have washed their robes in the blood of the Lamb.

The blood of the Lamb! the figure to which we are called, which is the fountain of love, that we are all to plunge into, so that we can become pure within and without, ready to appear in the wedding garments, and sit together and feast with the Lord, the Saviour, and the King of heaven and of earth!

> Then the song of the angels
> Shall greet our ear,
> And hosanna to God in the highest
> Shall be sung. We are then home,—
> Home for evermore with our loved ones
> And our Maker, God.

THE END.

Juvenile Publications

OF

J. B. LIPPINCOTT & CO.,

PHILADELPHIA.

For sale by all Booksellers, or will be sent by mail, postage free, on receipt of price.

ARTHUR'S ALL'S FOR THE BEST SERIES. In handsome box, containing: All's for the best; Heroes of the Household; The Seen and the Unseen. By T. S. ARTHUR. 3 vols. 16mo. Illustrated. Extra cloth. $2.25.

ARTHUR'S NEW JUVENILE LIBRARY. In box, containing: Who is Greatest? The Poor Wood-Cutter; Mr. Haven't-Got-Time; The Wounded Boy; Uncle Ben's New-Year's Gift; Pierre, the Organ-Boy; Who are Happiest? Maggie's Baby; The Peacemakers; The Lost Children; Our Harry; The Last Penny. By T. S. ARTHUR. 12 vols. With seventy-two Illustrations. Cloth, gilt back. $7.50.

BOYS' GLOBE LIBRARY. (FIRST SERIES.) In handsome box, containing: Sandford and Merton; Robinson Crusoe; The Arabian Nights' Entertainments; The Swiss Family Robinson. 4 vols. 12mo. Each with six Steel Plates printed in colors. Extra cloth. $6.00.

J. B. L. & CO.'S JUVENILE PUBLICATIONS.

BOYS' GLOBE LIBRARY. (Second Series.) In handsome box, containing: Pictures of Heroes, and Lessons from their Lives; Forty-four Years of a Hunter's Life; Fighting the Flames; Old Deccan Days, or Hindoo Fairy Legends. 4 vols. 12mo. With numerous Illustrations. Extra cloth. $6.00.

CHAMBERS'S LIBRARY FOR YOUNG PEOPLE. (First Series.) In box, containing: Alfred in India; Duty and Affection; Fireside Amusements; Grandmamma's Pocket; Moral Courage; Old England, a Tale; History of Scotland; Swan's Egg; Truth and Trust; Self-Denial; Clever Boys, and other Stories; History of England; History of France; Little Robinson; Orlandino; Poems for Young People; Steadfast Gabriel, a Tale; True Heroism, and other Stories; Uncle Sam's Money-Box; The Whisperer. 20 vols. 16mo. With twenty Engravings on Steel. Extra cloth, gilt back. $10.00.

CHAMBERS'S LIBRARY FOR YOUNG PEOPLE. (Second Series.) In box, containing: Alice Errol, and other Tales; My Birthday Book; Tales and Songs for Young Singers; Midsummer at Hay Lodge; Voices of Spring Flowers; Little Museum-Keepers; Wild Flowers and their Uses. 7 vols. 16mo. With seven Illustrations. Extra cloth, gilt back. $3.50.

CAMEOS FROM ENGLISH HISTORY. From Rollo to Edward II. By the author of "The Heir of Redclyffe." With Marginal Index. 12mo. Tinted paper. Cloth. $1.25. Extra cloth. $1.75.

"History is presented in a very attractive and interesting form for young folks in this work."—*Pittsburg Gazette.*
"An excellent design happily executed."—*N. Y. Times.*

CAST UP BY THE SEA. A book for Boys from Eight Years Old to Eighty. By Sir Samuel W. Baker, author of "The Albert N'Yanza," etc. With ten Illustrations by Huard, and Vignette Title. 12mo. Toned paper. Cloth. 75 cents. Fine edition. Extra cloth. $1.25.

J. B. L. & CO.'S JUVENILE PUBLICATIONS.

CASELLA; or, The Children of the Valleys. By MARTHA FARQUHARSON, author of "Elsie Dinsmore," etc. 16mo. Cloth. $1.50.

"A lively and interesting story, based upon the sufferings of the pious Waldenses, and is well written and life-like."—*Boston Chr. Era.*
"It is rich in all that is strong, generous, and true."—*Baltimore Episc. Methodist.*
"The story is one of the most interesting in ecclesiastical History."—*The Methodist.*

DEEP DOWN. A Tale of the Cornish Mines. By R. M. BALLANTYNE, author of "Fighting the Flames," "Silver Lake," etc. With Illustrations. *Globe Edition.* 12mo. Fine cloth. $1.50

"'Deep Down' can be recommended as a story of exciting interest, which boys will eagerly read, and which will give some valuable ideas on a subject about which very little is generally known. The book is embellished with a number of very excellent designs."—*Phila. Ev. Telegraph.*
"The author, through the attractive medium of a well-told story, has managed to give a vast amount of valuable information within a limited space."—*N. Y. Ev. Mail.*

ELSIE MAGOON; or, The Old Still-House. A Temperance Tale. Founded upon the actual experience of every-day life. By MRS. FRANCES D. GAGE. 12mo. Cloth. $1.50.

ERLING THE BOLD. A Tale of the Norse Sea-Kings. By R. M. BALLANTYNE, author of "Fighting the Flames," "Deep Down," etc. *Globe Edition.* With Illustrations. 12mo. Extra cloth. $1.50.

FEW FRIENDS (A), And How They Amused Themselves. A Tale in Nine Chapters, containing Descriptions of Twenty Pastimes and Games, and a Fancy-Dress Party. By MARY E. DODGE, author of "Hans Brinker," etc. 12mo. Extra cloth. $1.25.

"In the name of many readers, seniors as well as juniors, we thank Mrs. Dodge for a very pleasant and fascinating volume, which cannot fail to be in great demand during the holidays."—*Phila. Press.*
"It is not only useful but entertaining, and just the thing for holiday parties."—*Boston Advertiser.*

J. B. L. & CO.'S JUVENILE PUBLICATIONS.

FIGHTING THE FLAMES. A Tale of the London Fire Brigade. By R. M. BALLANTYNE, author of "Silver Lake," "The Coral Islands," etc. With Illustrations. *Globe Edition.* 12mo. Fine cloth. $1.50.

"An interesting and spirited little work."—*Phila. Ev. Telegraph.*

FORTY-FOUR YEARS OF A HUNTER'S LIFE. Being Reminiscences of Meshach Browning, a Maryland Hunter. With numerous Illustrations. *Globe Edition.* 12mo. Fine cloth. $1.50.

"It is a book which will be read with the greatest avidity by thousands in all sections of the country; and we rejoice in the belief that the worthy old hunter will be cheered, before he closes his earthly career, with a substantial recompense."—*Baltimore American.*

FUZ-BUZ AND MOTHER GRABEM. The Wonderful Stories of Fuz-Buz the Fly and Mother Grabem the Spider. A Fairy Tale. Handsomely illustrated. Small 4to. Cloth. $1.00. Extra cloth, gilt top. $1.25.

"Laughable stories, comically illustrated for little folks. The very book to delight little boys and girls. Get it for the holidays."—*Pittsburg Chronicle.*

LITTLE ONES' LIBRARY. In box, containing: A Gift for the Little Ones at Home; Nursery Songs and Rhymes; The Lily; Little Pet's Book; The Dew-Drop; The Faithful Dog; Grandfather's Visit; The Pet Lamb; Songs and Stories; The Widow's Cottage; The Pet Squirrel; The Home Story Book. With numerous Illustrations. 12 vols. 18mo. Cloth, gilt back. $4.00. Paper covers. $1.60.

QUAKER PARTISANS (THE). An exciting Story of the Revolution. By the author of "The Scout." With Illustrations. 12mo. Fine cloth. $1.50.

"It is a story of stirring incidents turning upon the actual movements of the war, and is told in an animated style of narrative which is very attractive. Its handsome illustrations will still further recommend it to the young people."—*New York Times.*

J. B. L. & CO.'S JUVENILE PUBLICATIONS.

MAN UPON THE SEA; or, A History of Maritime Adventure, Exploration, and Discovery, from the Earliest Ages to the Present Time. With numerous Engravings. By FRANK B. GOODRICH, author of "The Court of Napoleon," etc. 8vo. Cloth. $2.25.

"This eloquent and well-illustrated volume contains a large amount of rare and interesting information, conveyed in an easy and very pleasant style."—*Boston Recorder.*

"By its judicious selection of topics, its skilful condensation, and its agreeable style, it is adapted to supply the place in the library of no small number of voluminous and costly works."—*New York Tribune.*

"The book will be warmly welcomed by young people."—*Boston Post.*

OLD DECCAN DAYS; or, Hindoo Fairy Legends current in Southern India. Collected from oral tradition by M. FRERE. With an Introduction and Notes by Sir BARTLE FRERE. *Globe Edition.* 12mo. Illustrated. Fine cloth. $1.50.

"This little collection of Hindoo Fairy Legends is probably the most interesting book extant on that subject. * * * The stories of this little book are told in a very lively and agreeable style,—a style few writers of English possess, but which, when it belongs to a lady, is the best and most attractive in the world."—*N. Y. Times.*

OUR OWN BIRDS; or, A Familiar Natural History of the Birds of the United States. By WILLIAM L. BAILY. Revised and Edited by EDWARD D. COPE, Member of the Academy of Natural Sciences. With full Index. With numerous Illustrations. 16mo. Toned paper. Extra cloth. $1.50.

"To the youthful, 'Our Own Birds' is likely to prove a bountiful source of pleasure, and cannot fail to make them thoroughly acquainted with the birds of the United States. As a science there is none more agreeable to study than ornithology. We therefore feel no hesitation in commending this book to the public. It is neatly printed and bound, and is profusely illustrated."—*New York Herald.*

RIFLE AND HOUND IN CEYLON. Hunting Adventures in Ceylon. By Sir SAMUEL W. BAKER, author of "Cast Up by the Sea," etc. With Illustrations. 12mo. Fine cloth. $1.50.

J. B. L. & CO.'S JUVENILE PUBLICATIONS.

SILVER LAKE; or, Lost in the Snow. By R. M. BALLANTYNE, author of "The Wild Man of the West," "Fighting the Flames," etc. With Illustrations. Square 12mo. Tinted paper. Extra cloth. $1.25.

"We heartily recommend the book, and can imagine the pleasure many a young heart will receive on its perusal."—*The Eclectic Review.*

TALKS WITH A CHILD. Talks with a Child on the Beatitudes. Second edition. 18mo. Extra cloth. 75 cents. Flexible cloth. 50 cents.

"A volume written in a sweet, devout, simple, and tender spirit, and calculated to edify the old as well as the young."—*Boston Ev. Trans.*

TREES, PLANTS, AND FLOWERS: Where, and How they Grow. By WILLIAM L. BAILY, author of "Our Own Birds," etc. With seventy-three Engravings. 16mo. Toned paper. Extra cloth.

TUTOR'S COUNSEL (A). En Avant, Messieurs! Being a Tutor's Counsel to his Pupils. By the Rev. G. H. D. MATHIAS, M.A. 16mo. Fine cloth. $1.50.

"Every page of the book contains matter that will profit not only the young, but the old."—*Boston Com'l Bulletin.*

www.ingramcontent.com/pod-product-compliance
Lightning Source LLC
Chambersburg PA
CBHW022137160426
43197CB00009B/1330